THROUGH THE LEI

THE TYPHOON A1 ....

A PICTORIAL TRIBUTE

The lack of performance at altitude prevented the Hawker Typhoon from being one of the great fighters of the Second World War. It was to excel, however, in the ground attack role against enemy tanks and railways. (By kind permission of the RAF Museum, P100408)

KEN RIMELL

To find out about other titles produced by Historic Military Press visit our website at www.historicmilitarypress.com. Alternatively please write to us free of charge at: Customer Services, Historic Military Press, Freepost SEA 11014, Pulborough, West Sussex, RH20 4BR, or telephone our freephone number: 0800 071 7419.

HISTORIC MILITARY PRESS

THE TYPHOON AT WAR
A PICTORIAL TRIBUTE
© Copyright Ken Rimell, 2002.

First published 2002 by Historic Military Press,
ISBN 1-901313-14-X

ACKNOWLEDGMENTS

In writing this book I am indebted to the many Typhoon pilots, and their faithful ground crews, who allowed me free access to their private wartime albums of pictures. They were also generous of their time in telling me their stories with many, at first, very reluctant to do so.

It would be wrong of me therefore to list any specific people since everyone was so helpful. But I needed confirmation for captioning. It's unfair to ask for exact details after an elapse of 50 plus years since the war and we found that even the odd pilots' log book was wrong as well.

So in an effort to be as accurate as possible I have used a few excellent books, by way of cross reference, among them is Chris Thomas's Typhoon and Tempest Story, which is the established bible of matters Typhoon and Tempest, and several titles from flying legend, Wing Commander Roland Beamont - after all he did fly in combat and test both types. Group Captain Des Scott's two books, One Hour More and Typhoon Pilot, both give a raw account and no frills experience of the Typhoon and Tempest in action. To John Golley's excellent Day of The Typhoon, his own personal account of flying the aircraft with No. 245 Squadron and his personal credit to me in his final chapter.

But my final thanks must go to the late Air Chief Marshal Sir Harry Broadhurst and his wife Lady Jane who invited me to their Chichester home almost on a fortnightly basis. They shared an interest in our museum and indeed donated many things to it over the years. Our 'chats' would go on for hours lubricated by copious supplies of tea and cakes served from a silver tea set and the very best platters.

Sir Harry or 'Broadie' as he was affectionately known, would not suffer fools gladly so I failed to see where he went wrong in giving me such a vast amount of his time. I was privileged to serve under him in RAF Bomber Command in the 1960's on the mighty Vulcan Bombers, albeit as a junior NCO. In the later part of the 1960's I had been demobbed and he had retired from the RAF and we found ourselves at a Hawker function at Dunsfold Aerodrome near Cranleigh in Surrey where Harrier Jump Jets were under construction. From then on, we kept in touch, at first every few months but latterly on a more regular basis.

Both are now dead and with their departure goes an era that will never be repeated.

Unless indicated, all the photographs and relics shown in this book come from the author's collection. We are also grateful to the Royal Air Force Museum at Hendon, for allowing us to reproduce the photographs on the cover and title page.

Front Cover: It was intended that the Hawker Typhoon should enter service as an interceptor fighter in July 1940. Problems with the Napier Sabre engine, however, delayed its entry into service until 1941, when it became the first RAF aircraft capable of flying at 400 mph. (By kind permission of the RAF Museum, Hendon, P100407)

Printed in the United Kingdom by DC Data Systems, 95 Poulters Lane, Worthing, West Sussex, BN14 7SY Tel: 01903 525 695

HISTORIC MILITARY PRESS
Green Arbor, Rectory Road, Storrington, West Sussex, RH20 4EF. Telephone/Fax: 01903 741941
www.historicmilitarypress.com.

The Typhoon at War
A Pictorial Tribute.

In everyone's life there exists a certain regret, mine is never seeing a Typhoon or Tempest fly. By the time I was out of nappies the new range of RAF fighters, such as Vampires, Venoms and Meteors where now skimming across the skies. Holding my mother's hand as we trudged the mile or so to infants school, I was blissfully unaware that huge mounds of Hawker Typhoons, and a few Tempests, were scattered on airfields across the south. Their war service now done, they were awaiting the death sentence and the final swing of the scrapman's axe.

The Typhoon, whose development commenced in 1937, had an early life that could easily be described as a disaster. The prototype, which first flew on the 24th February 1940, revealed a design that some called an 'ugly duckling'. Furthermore, the desperate need at that time for front-line fighters, such as the Hurricane and Spitfire, increased pressure on both Hawker and the design team. After much painful development, including a number of crashes and the deaths of a number of test pilots, production finally started in 1941. Squadron Nos. 56 and 609 began re-equipping with the type at Duxford in September of that year.

However, problems persisted, and there was even talk of scrapping the entire programme. There were engine seizures - the mighty and complicated Napier Sabre, a new breed of sleeve valve engine was far more powerful than any other aero engine of the time. Then there were exhaust gases entering the open cockpit, a fault that killed several pilots before the cause was discovered. The first to be killed in this manner was Pilot Officer J. Deck who died in November 1941 whilst flying out of Duxford. Deck had been a pilot with No.56 Squadron - the first to get the Typhoon, and was one of three brothers to join the RAF. All three were pilots, and all were sadly to be killed in combat. Two are buried in the family plot in Suffolk, whilst an empty plot stands alongside awaiting the third brother. He had been killed almost as peace was declared flying Tempests over Europe - his body has yet to be found.

The losses during development continued. The Gloster

Aircraft Company's chief test pilot, Gerry Sayer, and another test pilot in a second aircraft, were both killed in the course of the same test flight. The cause has never been established as neither the aircraft nor the pilot's bodies have ever been found. On the 11th August 1942, Hawker's test pilot, Ken Seth-Smith was killed when his Typhoon crashed near Staines in Middlesex.

Other pilots escaped such incidents, thankfully surviving to pass on details of their experiences. One such test pilot was Hawker's employee Philip Lucas. His Typhoon experienced the worst problem to befall the types' development - structural failure along the tail. Lucas was able to guide his aircraft home after the tail on his Typhoon failed whilst recovering from a dive. Having landed, it was found that the tail was hanging on by a few shreds of airframe. For his skillful flying, Lucas was awarded a well deserved George Medal.

Fortunately, perseverance paid off, and gradually the faults were overcome. One of the most outspoken supporters of the Typhoon was Wing Commander Bee Beamont. On rest from combat flying, and testing for Hawkers, he indicated to the Air Chiefs, who were considering cancelling the project, that this was a fine aircraft and might be better suited for another type of role - that of high speed low level bomb or rocket attack.

By November 1942 this single seat fighter-bomber

had begun to prove its worth, showing that it was capable of catching and destroying the fastest fighter-bombers in the Luftwaffe which were then making hit-and-run attacks across the Channel. In 1943 "Tiffy" Squadrons engaged and destroyed anything that moved in Northern France and the Low Countries. In the lead up to, during, and after the D-Day landings the Typhoon spread fear through German ground forces. Capable of round the clock operations from poor quality advanced airfields, the Typhoon poured millions of cannon shells, rockets and heavy bombs into German ground forces. In one day alone, Typhoons knocked out 175 German tanks in the Falaise Gap. The Summer of 1944 was without doubt the types finest hour, and when, most historians will agree, the Typhoon proved its value to the Allied war effort.

Not a great deal has been written about this first class aircraft. Indeed what has gone before has generally dealt with its development and squadron allocations. Several Typhoon and Tempest pilots have written their own tribute, and published books, but only one other that I know has given any importance to pictures.

Hugh Halliday's book, published a few years ago, deals with the Canadians who flew Typhoons, either with their own squadrons or those who flew with the RAF. It is not a purely pictorial account but does have an interesting array of photographs. It is my intention to make this book a pictorial account brought about by the huge collection of pictures given to me over the years by those who either flew or worked on these magnificent machines. It is, in effect, a tribute to both the machine and the men who flew them.

Ken Rimell

THE AUTHOR

Ken Rimell is an established military historian, and has been the author of a number of previous books on military subjects. He has long held an interest in the military aviation history of the Second World War, and in particular its links with the County of Sussex. Ken is also renowned for his interest in military fire engines, the work of RAF Air Sea Rescue launches, and aircraft and the events surrounding D-Day. Ken is also the co-owner of the fascinating D-Day Aviation Museum, originally established at the one time advanced landing ground (ALG) at Apuldram, near Chichester, but now located at Shoreham Airport in Sussex.

An impressive shot of a 'clean' Typhoon on air test, clearly showing the four 20-mm wing-mounted cannon that formed a valuable part of the Typhoon's armoury. The pilot on this occasion was Peter Cadbury.

The Typhoon prototype first flew on the 24th February 1940 and marked the start of an almost disastrous development programme. This picture, taken at Hawker's factory at Langley in 1940, shows the restricted rear view afforded to the pilot. Later improved variants had the bubble canopy with clear all round vision.

The Typhoon cockpit and instrument layout - often called 'the office'.

Above: A Napier Sabre engine under destruction testing at Napier's own Engine Test Facility at Acton in London. Ducting has been fitted to the exhaust stubs to remove the fumes from the building. Initially the Sabre was an unreliable powerplant, providing a poor rate of climb and weak performance at higher altitudes. Nevertheless, with the help of test beds such as that shown, important improvements were made that eventually allowed the Typhoon to excel as a low level, high speed fighter-bomber.

Centre right: Flight tests were an integral part of the development of both the Sabre engine and the Typhoon as a whole. This photograph shows Jock Bonnar, a former Napier test pilot, who was responsible for testing the Typhoon's Sabre engines. For his work he was later awarded the George Medal.

Bottom: Perhaps the greatest fault that befell the Typhoon was a weakness along the tail area. Indeed the problem was so serious, causing the death of a number of test pilots, that the Typhoon project was nearly cancelled. The 'fishplates,' shown here just forward of the tail, were one attempt at curing any further tail breakages. The actual reason for the failures was not discovered until after the war - resonance at the aircraft's weakest point.

Left: Fitters replacing the mighty Napier Sabre engine in a Typhoon. A well practised team such as this could have the task done in 10 hours. The 24 cylinder Sabre engine, capable of developing 2,180-hp, was to cause a number of problems during the development of the Typhoon.

Below: The clean lines of another Typhoon that is about to go on an air test. The location of this picture is unknown, though the buildings in the back ground might provide someone with the necessary clues.

Opposite Top: Douglas Oram of No.174 Squadron poses by his aircraft. This is an early production example of the Typhoon - evidenced by the 'car-type' door for the cockpit entrance. Gloster built 3,315 of the 3,330 Typhoons completed, with the final 3,000 or so examples having a clear bubble hood instead of a heavy-framed 'car-type' door, which, incidentally, was fitted on both sides of the cockpit.

Opposite Bottom: The same aircraft as in the previous photograph following unexplained engine failure. Thankfully Douglas Oram walked away unscathed from the crash.

Note the liberally sprayed engine oil over the propellers and engine cowling. Could this be indicative of a catastrophic failure within the Napier unit?

Left: Wing Commander Roland Beamont poses for the camera in front of his aircraft. While on rest from operational flying he was invited to test fly Typhoons for Hawkers.

In spite of many earlier problems it was his faith in the aircraft that convinced the War Office to continue using it. As a result it was to become one of the greatest ground attack aircraft ever built.

Middle: Another early 'car-door' type Typhoon pictured during a patrol. This No.609 Squadron example is being flown by Mac MacKennaugh.

Bottom: With flaps and wheels down, and with rocket rails empty, Johnny Buttons lands this No.174 Squadron Typhoon after a successful attack on an enemy target.

Two of the New Zealand pilots from No.486 Squadron chat at Tangmere during the summer of 1944. On the left is Frank Murphy, who after the war became a Hawker test pilot, whilst on the right is Allan Smith. Note that they both wear 'New Zealand' shoulder titles.

Indicating a successful attack Squadron Leader Dennis Crowley-Milling, of No.181 Squadron, 'shoots a line' to his assembled pilots. Directly in front and wearing a 'German Cross', (taken from a German pilot P.O.W. after being shot down over Kent), is 'Fin' Haddock who was later shot down and escaped. He was on the run for three months until captured by the Gestapo and tortured. After the war he became a doctor.

The pilots of No.266 (Rhodesia) Squadron line up in front of one of the Squadrons Typhoons at Exeter in 1943. No.266 Squadron was first formed on the 27th September 1918, remaining in service until finally disbanded in June 1964.

Typhoon legend Group Captain Des Scott, (standing with his arms folded in the centre), with the pilots from his Squadron - No.486 Squadron, (RNZAF). The sheer size of the Typhoon is clearly evident in this picture.

Above: A group photograph showing the pilots of No.181 Squadron in front of one of their Typhoons. Commanded by Squadron Leader Dennis Crowley-Milling, this picture was taken at Snailwall in February 1943.

Bottom Left: Not all landings were executed in an orderly fashion. Here we see the results of a wheels-up landing - one rather bent and forlorn Typhoon. It was, however, repaired and later flew again.

Bottom Right: This No.137 Squadron Typhoon clearly shows the Typhoon's firepower. Fully loaded, the Typhoon could carry eight rockets or two 500lb (later 1,000lb) bombs - alongside the Hispano Cannon of course. These weapons were what enabled the Typhoon to so capably carry out its role of high speed, low level fighter-bomber.

A group picture, taken before a mission, shows a fully armed Typhoon of No.198 Squadron. The pilot of this particular aircraft, Howard Morley, is on the extreme right.

Below: A group photograph from No.175 Squadron. No.175 Squadron had a relatively brief life, being formed on the 3rd March 1942, and disbanded on the 30th September 1945. On the left-hand of the front row, standing behind the Alastian, is Osmond Kelsick. Kelsick, (insert), from the West Indies, was later awarded the DFC whilst flying with the Squadron.

Pictured in the winter of 1943/1944, this No.197 Squadron Typhoon is about to start up and take off on an air test. JP504 is one of the early production examples.

Another group photograph - this time from No.198 Squadron, though the subjects seem more interested in something other than the cameraman! The picture was taken in February 1944 whilst the Squadron was based at Manston in Kent - an ideal base from which to launch low-level strikes across the French mainland. It is with much sadness that one notes that by the time the war ended, over half of these men would have been killed in action - 11 out of 20. Five nationalities are also represented - British, Canadian (including one French-Canadian), Australian, New Zealand and Belgian.

Two pictures showing an aircraft of No.245 Squadron at RAF Gravesend in the spring of 1943. They depict the Typhoon flown by Flying Officer Sam Slaney, an American serving with the Squadron. Above: Here the armourers are adding their own message to one of the bombs - 'From me to you Adolf'! The wording along the side of the engine cowling reads 'Northern Rhodesia Squadron', indicating an aircraft from this Squadron. The second of these two pictures, below, shows the armourers actually bombing up the same aircraft. The original hand written caption read "Jimmy Wilson's 'M' for Mike. The only thing that ever worked on that aeroplane was the brake on the control column", (this aircraft was later flown by another No.245 Squadron pilot, Jimmy Wilson).

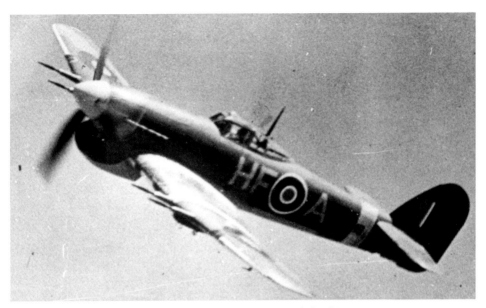

Above: Albert Collins, No.183 Squadron, reforms on his leader, who took the picture.

Below: Another shot of a No.181 Squadron Typhoon - this time on the ground surrounded by some of the Squadron's pilots. The picture was taken in May 1943 whilst No.181 was based at Tangmere. Note will be made of one of the pilots pictured, F/Lt Richard Guthrie, who can be seen sitting at the back between the spaniel and the exhaust stubs. Guthrie was killed in action soon after D-Day on the 18th August 1944. He is buried at Bayeux Cemetery, France.

No.197 Squadron pilots: from left to right, John Rook, Dumbo Taylor (killed June 1944), Hank Jones (killed December 1944), and Bruce Gilbert.

Typhoon pilots being briefed on an airfield in the south on D-Day itself. From this moment on the Typhoon was to be one of the most formidable weapons available to the Allied invasion forces. The briefing, led by Squadron Leader Butch Taylor of No.197 Squadron, is thought to be taking place at Holsley South in the New Forest.

How not to land a Typhoon! This aircraft, from No.195 Squadron, crashed on approach to Woodvale on the 19th March 1943. The pilot Sgt. F. Jones survived the crash of DN474.

In the panoramic picture one can see how the wreckage has spread across a small part of a golf course, with the tail section (centre) ending upside down just off the green.

The third picture, taken at the time, shows how many a Typhoon pilot might have responded to the crash - here no evil, speak no evil, see no evil!

19

Right: A happy group of pilots from No.197 Squadron pictured in late 1943. Unfortunately the happiness was not to last. Fibber McFee was shot down and became a POW. Bob Jones was killed in December 1943, and Nobby Clark in July 1944. Meanwhile, Jerry MaHaffey was shot down on November 24th 1943 near Dunkirk, escaped, was picked up and resumed flying with the squadron later the same day.

Below: No.193 'Fellowship of the Bellows' Squadron was formed on the 18th December 1942. Here is a line up of the original Squadron members in a photograph taken at Harrowbeer, Devon, in January 1943. Left to right are (surnames only) Ray; Switzer; Davidge; Samuels; Dunsmuir; Thorne; Orlebar; Kirkpatrick; Jones; Beake; Petre (OC); Crabb; Webb; Inglis; MacDonald; McKay; Lawson; Lawston; McCartney; Plows and Brown.

No.245 'North Rhodesia' Squadron Typhoons pictured at the Advanced Landing Ground at Selsey on a wet and windy day in 1943. Note the Hurricane in the background.

Another Typhoon pictured on D-Day itself. This No.175 Squadron Typhoon, flown by John Henry, is seen between missions at the New Forest Airfield, Holmsley South. One could assume that the aircraft is in the process of being re-armed, judging by the rockets arranged on the ground behind the fuselage.

Above: Three No.198 Squadron pilots who are, from left to right, Flying Officers Wing, Peter Roper, and Dennis Sweeting. Roper was to have an incredible experience after crashing in France. With a badly smashed leg, Roper was taken to the home of a local French aristocrat, who even today only wishes to be known as 'The Count'. The Count helped an unknown number of RAF pilots by sheltering them in his chateau before handing them on to the escape networks of the French resistance.

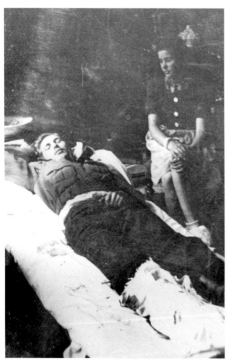

The picture on the left is somewhat remarkable, and indeed was not seen by Roper himself until 1986 when Roper, the author and other former Typhoon pilots were invited to the Count's Chateau in France. Taken by the Count himself, it shows a female member of the French Resistance tending Roper and his injuries whilst being sheltered in the Chateau. Having been repatriated, the third photograph of Roper, (below), is another incredible find - this time by the author. It shows Roper appearing in an official British propaganda film, intended to demonstrate how quickly wounded pilots recover after crashing.

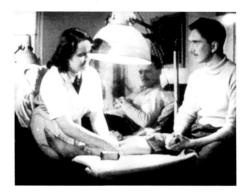

Left: On March 14th 1944 Peter Sewell, (seen here on the right), experienced an engine failure while on a Typhoon delivery flight to Tangmere. His aircraft crashed through the kitchen of a house not far from the airfield boundary, breaking both of his legs. With him is the current owner of the house former RAF Meteor pilot and latterly a Virgin 'Jumbo' skipper, Dennis Shrosbree.

Below: As soon as possible after the 6th June 1944, Typhoon Squadrons were despatched across the Channel to forward airbases in an effort to provide as close support as was viable to the invasion armies. Here, having just arrived in Normandy is a No.181 Squadron Typhoon. By now many allied pilots were wearing army style khaki uniforms, as several had been mistakenly shot at by French Resistance workers, as well as British and other Allied soldiers. It was found that the airmen's blue uniform was too similar to that of the Luftwaffe. By late June the black and white invasion stripes had been removed from the aircraft's top surfaces.

To enable the new forward airfields to be established quickly on French soil, they were kept as basic and as simple as possible. Here, rocket armed Typhoons roll along a metal 'mesh' tracking just prior to taking off.

There can be no doubt that the Typhoon packed quite a punch. By D-Day, utilisation of the Typhoon was at its peak, with no fewer than 26 Squadrons serving in the 2nd TAF (Tactical Air Force). An attack by a Typhoon Squadron was often disastrous for any German Unit that received such attentions. One Canadian reporter gave the following description: "Burned out tanks and vehicles in incredible numbers lined and blocked every road and track. Dead soldiers and horses, by hundreds and thousands, lay on the roadways and ditches. Bulldozers had to clear a way through the debris for our advancing columns". The French village in this picture was reported as having been full of German troops. The result was a visit by Typhoons from the 2nd TAF. The insert shows the same high street today.

Here pilots from No.174 Squadron have just landed in France, on June 18th 1944, and are setting up camp on a hastily prepared advanced landing ground near Bayeux. A 'battlefield briefing', for an attack on an unspecified enemy target, is in progress whilst the aircraft are refueled and rearmed with rockets, cannon shells and bombs.

Below: The rocket projectiles carried on the Typhoon were often used to devasting effect. Ron Grant, on the right, shows fellow pilots the damage that his patrol inflicted on a German Headquarters building in Normandy in early July 1944. Grant was later shot down and taken prisoner. His official P.O.W. papers are shown here in the insert (left).

Above: Typhoon pilots having fun in an armoured personnel carrier. Having suffered a seized engine, the British Army abandoned the vehicle in France in the weeks after the invasion. Following the attentions of a number of Typhoon fitters it was soon up and running again, and put to use as a Squadron transport.

Right: Pilots of No.175 Squadron, on an advanced landing ground in Normandy. Pictured on the 20th June 1944, and with full messing facilities not yet in place, the pilots have devised their own method of cooking. This contraption was known as 'The Jarvis Inferno' after its inventor, Flying Officer Ted Jarvis, used aviation fuel to get it started.

Above: No.198 Squadron pilots watch whilst their CO, Paul Ezzano, feeds a pet rabbit in a captured German helmet. The tented accommodation in the background is typical of that found on the forward airfields established in France after D-Day. On the extreme left is Flt.Sgt. Reg Thursby who was, sadly, later shot down and killed. Like Ace Miron, (see page 28), his body was found 50 years after he crashed and was buried at St. Charles de Percy Cemetery, France.

Above: This unfortunately poor quality photograph shows pilots from No.146 Wing. In particular, on the third from the left, is Wing Commander Reg Baker. Whilst flying from RAF Needs Oar Point, near Beaulieu in Hampshire, on June 16th 1944 he was shot down by flak. His Typhoon crashed near Caen and he was killed. The second picture, (bottom left), shows the makeshift grave of Wing Commander Baker with the remains of his aircraft and a solitary propeller blade as its marker. It is known that advancing British soldiers had dug the grave.

Below: Squadron Leader T.S.Rumbold DFC, of No.263 Squadron, on an advanced landing ground in France, sporting a captured German helmet and rifle.

Above: This picture shows the grave of a Typhoon pilot in a private garden in France. The two former French Resistance men, pictured by it, were responsible for carrying out the dying pilot's wish to be buried there in 1944. After the war, and via the British Red Cross, the two men contacted the relatives of the dead pilot. They expressed a desire to see him remain where he had fallen, and so some years later the Commonwealth War Graves Commission granted a gravestone - a relatively unusual act. The picture was handed to the author in 1990. The grave is that of Pilot Officer Ernest George Boucher, of No.174 Squadron. Boucher was

shot down on the 5th of August 1944, aged just 21, and is buried at Caligny, France. (The full story can be found in a forthcoming publication "The D-Day Memorials").

Top Right: With time the German ground forces came to fear the arrival of the Typhoon flight. Such a reputation would also cause problems for any Typhoon pilots should they have the misfortune of crashing and being captured. Indeed, there are reports that some Germans took their feelings to the extreme. No.175 Squadron pilot Flight Sergeant Ronnie Dale was found by Allied soldiers having been bayoneted to death by the Germans. He is now buried in the military cemetery at Bayeux. Each year the author visits the grave.

Left: Fifty-five years after he was killed, the body of No.245 Squadron's Ace Miron was found in the remains of his Typhoon which had crashed in soft ground in Normandy on the 17th August 1944. He and Pilot Officer Thompson had attacked a German armoured convoy near Les Autels. The convoy received a mauling and the brace of Typhoons were just going in to finish the task when Miron was hit by flak. His Typhoon was seen to dive into the ground. Miron, a Canadian, was buried with full military honours at St. Charles de Percy Cemetery, Normandy.

A No.175 Squadron Mark IB Typhoon is prepared for a bombing mission and gets the 'going over' by the fitters and armourers (who are loading the 500lb bombs). This is yet another of the early 'car-door' Typhoons, and was almost certainly pictured well before D-Day. Despite this, the so-called 'invasion stripes', which did not generally appear until the 5th June 1944, are present. It was considered that the Typhoon could easily be mistaken for the German Focke-Wolf 190, and so the black and white stripes were introduced, for the Typhoon, in 1943.

A brace of No.137 Squadron Typhoons take off for a raid from Eindhoven, January 1945. The leading aircraft is flown by Ken Brain DFC.

Rocket tubes and fins await warheads at a captured German airfield in early 1945. Note the devastation caused by previous Allied air attacks and artillery fire from the advancing Allied armies.

Another view of Typhoons at Eindhoven in Holland. This Typhoon IB of No.137 Squadron is pictured in early 1945. Ken Brain DFC flew this particular aircraft. The Hurricane just visible beneath the Typhoon's wing was used as a Squadron hack until destroyed by the last major German fighter sweep of the war - note that this too, even as late as January 1945, is still sporting the black and white stripes.

Top left: Air Chief Marshal Sir Harry Broadhurst with Winston Churchill on VE Day 1945. Broadhurst, or "Broadie" as he was known, was basically the man in charge of the Typhoons during the Second World War - he commanded 83 Group which consisted of, mainly, Typhoon Squadrons. Its designated task was the support of the British Second Army. It was he who helped to ensure that these aircraft were used to such effect, forming a valuable part of the Allied fighting forces.

Top right: Even to this day, somewhat surprisingly, Typhoon bits can still be found scattered across Normandy. This was once a Typhoon rocket rail, though now serves as a fence post.

Below: The Hawker Typhoon's Napier Sabre engine. This one was dug up in France in 1987, albeit minus many of the smaller parts and carburettors. It is only because of a bent propeller boss that we have any indication that the aircraft had powered into soft ground, in 1944, at nearly 400mph.

Above: In 1986, members from No.175 Squadron gathered at the RAF Museum in Hendon, meeting for the first time since the Second World War. Here they are pictured alongside the only surviving Typhoon. From left to right they are: Peter Baden; Poppa Ambrose; Tommy Hall (who flew in from Australia); Jim Wood (from Canada); Mike Inglefinch; Jack Frost; Bill Speedie (again from Australia); and Frank McManus (another Canadian).

Below: The massed ranks of the first ever Typhoon and Tempest reunion. The lone lady in the foreground was an ATA, (Air Transport Association), pilot who delivered the Typhoons from the factory to the squadrons. Monique Agazarian went on to run her own air freight and flying school business from White Waltham after the war. The year is 1984 and the location - the former Sgts. Mess, RAF Tangmere.